Helping A Hero

by Jo S. Kittinger
Illustrated by Chuck Galey

Acknowledgments

Helping a Hero would not have been possible without the support and encouragement of many people. We want particularly to acknowledge the contributions of Ronald Grais, Mark Ishaug and their colleagues at Thresholds; Steve Scudder, Kelly Scott, Cheryl Zalenski, Bryan Kay and Tim Brandhorst of the American Bar Association; Ellen Lawton, the founding Executive Director of the National Center for Medical-Legal Partnership; Gale S. Pollock, Major General (Retired), former Surgeon General of the United States; and, Drs. John and Cynthia Csernansky, of the Feinberg School of Medicine at Northwestern University.

This book, the second in a series of books incorporating lessons of self-empowerment and legal literacy, embodies the unique vision and dedication of Tony Barash and Terri Hanson, and their colleagues, the Fellows, Faculty and Staff of the Harvard Advanced Leadership Initiative.

And, above all, we salute America's 21.5 million veterans, and we honor and thank them and their families for their service and their sacrifice.

Jo S. Kittinger
Chuck Galey

Summary: When a veteran struggles to re-enter society, his niece seeks the help of a medical-legal partner, who in turn connects him with a local social service agency specializing in helping veterans.

[1. U. S. Military veterans-Non-fiction. 2. Veterans of foreign wars-Non-fiction. 3. Legal Assistance-Non-fiction. 4. Medical-Legal Partnership-Non-fiction.]

"Hey, Bree, what's wrong?" I ask.

"Nothin'."

"Did your favorite uncle get moved in?"

"Uncle Jimmy went off to war," Bree says.

"Uncle Jim came back. It's hard to believe he's the same guy."

"What do you mean?" I ask. I kick the ball to Bree.

"Well, you met Uncle Jimmy before he left," Bree says. "He played soccer with us, was always laughing . . ."

"He was a lot of fun," I say. "What was it he called you? Oh yeah, it was Breezy."

"He hasn't called me that since he's been home. Come on over," Bree says. "You'll see the change."

Walking into their apartment, I accidentally slam the door.

I hear a thud and look over to see Uncle Jim on the floor.

He hustles to stand up and takes a drink from a can on the coffee table.

"He's a little jumpy," Bree whispers.

"Hi, Jim," I say.

But he just turns and stares out the window.

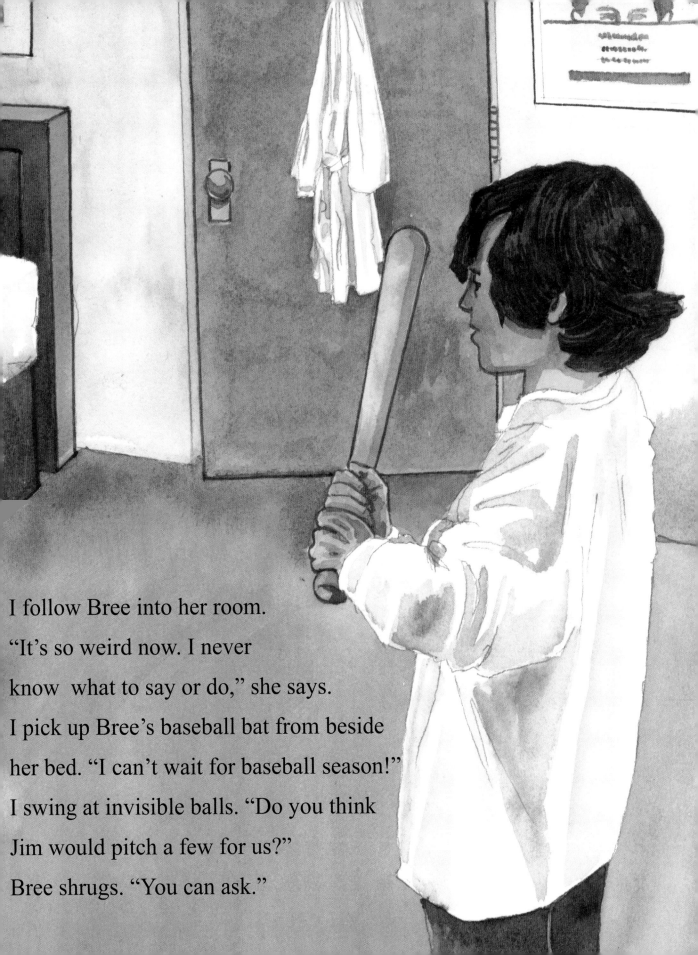

I follow Bree into her room.
"It's so weird now. I never
know what to say or do," she says.
I pick up Bree's baseball bat from beside
her bed. "I can't wait for baseball season!"
I swing at invisible balls. "Do you think
Jim would pitch a few for us?"
Bree shrugs. "You can ask."

"Okay. Sure," Jim says. "That might

be good."

But when we get downstairs to the

front door, Jim stops. He just

stands there, then takes two

steps back.

"You guys go on without

me," he says.

The next morning, I'm walking ChiChi when
Bree comes out with a bag of garbage.
"Jim won't even carry out the trash," she
complains.
"He woke up screaming with nightmares three
times last night. That guy needs help."

I lift the garbage can lid for Bree. "What kind of help?"
I ask.

"I don't know," Bree says. "He doesn't really want to
live with us, but he can't keep a job. Mom said she
doesn't know what to do."

"Hey, I know someone who helped our family. Maybe
she can help yours, too!"

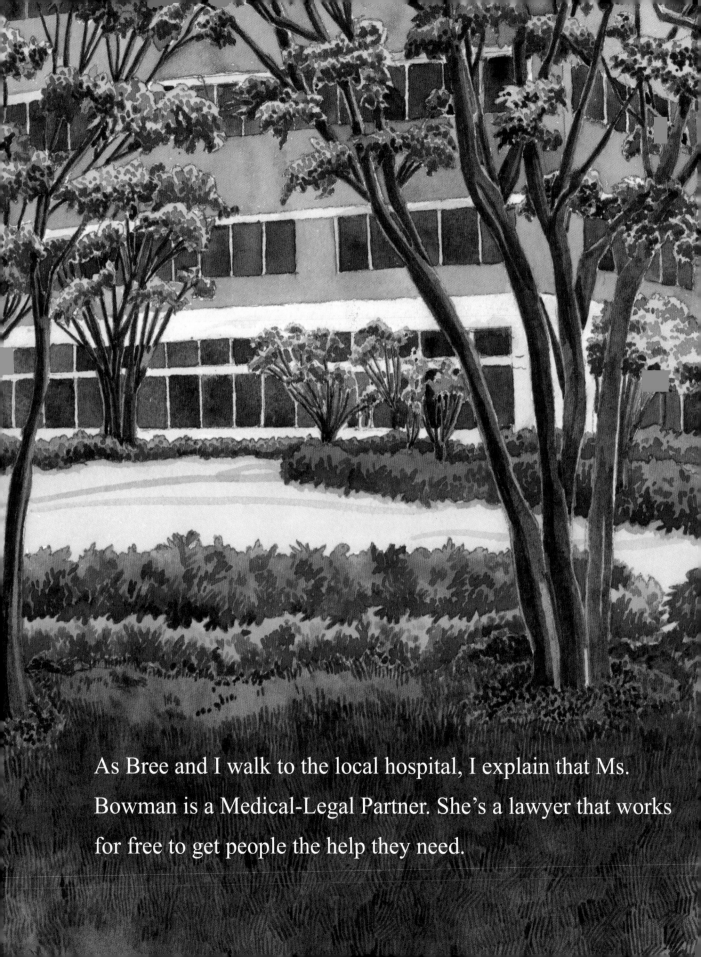

As Bree and I walk to the local hospital, I explain that Ms. Bowman is a Medical-Legal Partner. She's a lawyer that works for free to get people the help they need.

Ms. Bowman's door is open and she waves us in.

"Hi, Cristian!" she says. "How's your family?"

I explain that my family's great, but Bree's family needs help.

"Since my uncle came home from the war, he hasn't been able to keep a job," Bree says.

Ms. Bowman takes notes as Bree tells how her uncle has been acting.

"Can you help?" Bree asks.

Ms. Bowman smiles and takes Bree's hand. "I know people who can. There's a place called Thresholds. They have a Veterans' Project that helps struggling veterans find jobs and housing." Ms. Bowman promises to make some calls.

A few days later, Bree and I are playing a video game when Bree's mom gets home from work. Jim tells her the people from Thresholds called and asked to meet with him.

"But I know I need to be here to look after Bree," he says. "So, I can just tell them I can't come."

"I'll go with you!" Bree says. "Cristian can come too."

I thought we'd be going to some office, but Jim leads us into a coffee shop. A guy catches Jim's eye and waves us over. A beautiful dog lies at his feet.

"Can I pet her?" I ask.

"No, I'm sorry," the man says. "She's my assistance dog. She's working right now."

"Working?" I ask. "She looks like she's just lying there."

The dog looks up and thumps her tail on the floor.

"She's trained to keep me connected with real life. Lucy's been a big help since I got back from the war."

The man talks with Jim about a lot of stuff. But I can tell they're holding some stuff back, because Bree and I are there.

"Can we look in the toy store next door?" I ask. "We'll be back in about 15 minutes."

Jim nods and his eyes say "thank you."

When we come back, the man is saying, "Be patient, getting better takes time. But having an assisted job and an apartment of my own, made all the difference. That and Lucy, here." He rubs the dog's head.

As we wait, the man continues to talk about his dog and the ways she helps.

"Do you think my uncle could get an assistance dog?" Bree asks.

The man gives a command and the dog lies down. "There aren't enough dogs to go around, and they're pretty expensive. But some are donated. I got lucky, so I say go for it."

Jim stands and the man sticks out his
hand. "I'm sure we can get you into
a meaningful job," he says. Jim gives
him a tiny smile and a handshake.
"Come on Breezy, let's go home," Jim
says.

Back in Bree's room, she grins and gives
me a huge hug. "I think Uncle Jim may
be okay now. Thank you, Cristian!"
"And thank goodness for Ms. Bowman,"
I say.
"Now...." I hand Bree a pencil and notebook.
"How can we raise money to help Jim get
an assistance dog?"

Things You Should Know

Veterans Mental Health Services

The United States Veterans Administration offers a wide range of mental health services for veterans. If you are interested in learning more about mental health care available for veterans you will find a helpful Guide to VA Mental Health Services for Veterans & Families at http://www.mirecc.va.gov/MIRECC/VISN16/docs/Guide_to_VA_Mental_Health_Srvcs_FINAL12-20-10.pdf.

Thresholds

Thresholds is the largest and oldest provider of supported mental health services in Illinois, providing healthcare, housing, and hope for thousands of people with mental illness. Soldiers often return from combat with scars both physical and psychological. For many, reintegrating into their communities and their former lives proves impossible. Unable to cope, the tragic outcomes of homelessness, hopelessness, and helplessness are often the result. If you know a veteran from any war having a hard time coping with mental illness, trauma, or issues such as homelessness, substance abuse, employment or housing, learn more about Thresholds Veterans Project at http://www.thresholds.org/find-services/veterans-project.

For agencies providing supported mental health services in your community learn about the U.S. Psychiatric Rehabilitation Association at https://netforum.avectra.com/eWeb/StartPage.aspx?Site=USPRA&WebCode=HomePage.

Service Dogs

Veterans Moving Forward provides service dogs to veterans with physical and mental health challenges. Veterans and their families seeking assistance, service or skilled companion dogs can learn more at www.vetsfwd.org.

Medical-Legal Partnerships

Medical-legal partnerships (MLPS) put lawyers who provide free legal services into the healthcare setting to help patients and families solve problems that may be related to illness like access to housing and employment, public benefits for people with disabilities, and other areas of legal needs. For more information, go to the American Bar Association's Medical-Legal Partnership Pro Bono Support Project website at www.medlegalprobono.org and the National Center for Medical-Legal Partnership at http://www.medical-legalpartnership.org/.

Legal Aid

Legal Aid organizations are located in many cities and towns. They offer free or low-cost legal services to people who cannot afford to pay a lawyer. Often, there are special programs available for veterans and their families. You can search online for a Legal Aid organization in your area or ask a public librarian to help you locate these services. A directory of legal aid organizations can be found at www.findlegalhelp.org .